Dream Journal

Leon Nacson

Hay House, Inc.
Carlsbad, CA

Published and distributed in the United States by:
Hay House, Inc., P.O. Box 5100, Carlsbad, CA 92018-5100 • (800) 654-5126 • (800) 650-5115 (fax)

Researched and edited by: Rachel Eldred
Editorial supervision: Jill Kramer   Design: Christy Salinas   Illustration: Eris Klein

ISBN 1-56170-590-X

02 01 00 99   4 3 2 1
First Printing, July 1999

Printed in China

To Colleen—you are always on my mind.

I'd like to thank Rachel Eldred, Carol Floyd,
Christy Salinas, Jill Kramer, and Eris Klein
for their assistance in getting this project completed;
and also to Dr. Kal Thomas for his technical advice.

Contents

Foreword

by Louise L. Hay, bestselling author of *You Can Heal Your Life*

When I read through Leon's dream journal, I thought, *What a wonderful idea: a journal that reinforces the importance of the individual as the interpreter of their own dreams.* Whenever I am asked to help someone interpret a dream, I explain that the symbols in dreams are very much their own. Of course, I can tell you what the symbols mean to *me*, but I can't know if that is exactly what they mean to *you*. It's always best if you think about what the symbols mean in relation to your environment, your goals, and your beliefs. I think it is helpful to know that every part of your dream is a part of you, and if you give that part of you a voice, you can often figure out what is happening and what it means. This is what attracted me to Leon's dream journal—it encourages you to create your own personal treasure chest of dreams.

Creating a dream journal can be exciting. I believe that anyone can use it to help themselves heal and overcome challenges by focusing on something positive before drifting off to sleep. I like to go to sleep with gratitude. I go over the day, bless all the experiences I have had, and I am grateful. One thing I never do before I go to sleep is watch the evening news. I will not put anything overwhelming or overbearing in my consciousness before bed, because I believe that it seeps in and becomes a part of who I am.

With this dream journal, you are encouraged to ask key questions about your waking life that will help you individually determine just how much your environment affects your dream life. I know that whenever I am very upset or eat the wrong thing, I will often have a scary dream. My frightening dreams sometimes involve storm troopers chasing me. I'm just grateful they never quite catch me! Another unpleasant dream sees me with huge holes in my teeth. My favorite dreams, though, are flying dreams, and these usually parallel a high time in my life. It's clear to me that what is happening while I am awake affects my dream time.

What I also love about this dream journal is that you don't have to work on it for hours a day. I studied with a dream teacher once for about six months, and although it was an interesting journey, it got to the point where he wanted us to spend up to four hours a day on our dreams. It just got to be too much. With this dream journal, you are given the choice to spend as much time on your dreams as you like.

I treasure my dreams, and I encourage you to have as much fun as I've had unearthing their secrets.

With love,

Louise

Why Keep a Dream Journal?

Over the years, I've coached many people on how to interpret their dreams: personal dreams, erotic dreams, lucid dreams, prophetic dreams, insightful dreams, strange dreams—the list is endless. I can't think of anyone I've met who has not been intrigued by their dreams, and it's rare to come across someone who has had a strange or vivid dream and isn't interested in discussing it.

As a dream coach, I don't profess to hold the answers to what each and every symbol in your dream means. What I do have are tips on how you can interpret them. This involves showing an interest in all of your dream experiences, not just the occasional vivid dream. And what better way to encourage this interest than to keep a dream journal? A dream journal not only brings you closer to your dream world, but takes you on a journey toward greater self-discovery.

Imagine you are on the vacation of a lifetime, snapping photos of idyllic locations and fantastic places, only to return home to find there was no film in the camera! While parts of the experience are indelibly imprinted on your memory, the photos would have made the whole adventure easier to recall. It's the same with all those wonderful dreams you've had throughout life. How much easier would it be to recall, reexperience, and make use of your dreams if they were recorded?

A dream journal also provides a record of who you are. Just as a camera or a travel journal records an important journey in life, your dream journal helps to record *the* most important journey in life—your inner journey.

More important, a dream journal can open you up to a greater understanding of yourself. If you want to know why you feel the way you do, what will make you happier in life, or want to find out more about the people around you, a dream journal can help. Deciphering the language of the night will give you greater awareness and insight.

Continually reminded that you are a spiritual being having a human experience, life can be quite an adventure. Dreams enable you to explore your adventures in more detail. After you've been working with them for a while, you will notice that your intuition becomes more finely tuned, and this will help you clear up any confusion. (With over 60,000 thoughts swimming around in our head every day, it's little wonder we become confused!)

Improving your intuition is one of the greatest bonuses that results from keeping a dream journal. *Webster's Dictionary* defines intuition as "the power or faculty of attaining to direct knowledge or cognition without evident rational thought and inference." Intuition can be likened to a hand that gently guides and maneuvers you through life. And when you acknowledge and work with your dreams, you validate your intuition. You know that even though there may not be a scientific explanation for your dream, you still value its message and your intuitive understanding of it.

Regularly remind yourself that you are not trying to find definitive answers to your dreams; rather, you are opening yourself up to the associations, feelings, and thoughts that your dreams provoke. Dream interpretation does not have to be a scientific process where a strict formula is followed, but a brainstorming session where you let everything—your thoughts, feelings, and ideas—spew forth. As you write down your dreams, don't censor them or worry about grammar and spelling. You're not in pursuit of literary perfection; you're simply giving your intuition free rein to explore your mind.

When you first begin to write in your dream journal, you may feel uncomfortable with your thoughts and feelings, and you may tend to rely on others for validation. However, working with your dream journal is a solitary process—a way for you to establish an intimate bond with yourself.

This is why I advise, at least in the beginning, to avoid sharing your dreams with others. You don't want to be overly influenced by someone else's interpretations and explanations. This isn't to say you shouldn't share your dreams with someone at a later date; just give yourself a chance to make your own interpretations before you do so. Others may give us important insight and advice, but remember that nothing is gospel other than what you believe.

The longer you work with your dreams, the more intimate you will become with your own interpretations, and the less likely you will be to search for answers from others. Keeping a dream journal will strengthen your self-resolve. Like any relationship you work at, trust and faith will be fostered, and you will discover newfound freedom, confidence, and motivation.

Keeping a dream journal is also a perfect way to enhance self-awareness, the cornerstone to growth and change. Only when you are *aware* of your dreams, inspirations, strengths, and weaknesses, can you make the most informed choices. This doesn't mean that all your choices will be easy, but choosing will be easier. With greater self-awareness, growth is possible under any circumstances—whether they be pleasurable or painful—and you will be conscious of allowing that process to unfold.

Finally, keeping a dream journal should be fun. Not only will you find out more about your dreams, but you will delight in discovering more about yourself and how you move about in this world.

Ways to Use a Dream Journal

Now that you know the benefits of keeping a dream journal, read on to find out how you can utilize it for *maximum* benefit. The first few suggestions are general considerations to assist you when you're first starting out. As you become more familiar with keeping your dream journal, you might like to experiment with the final suggestions to really awaken your dreams.

1. Keep your journal in a safe place. Like a diary, your dream journal is a personal commentary about who you are. It will be a record of fantasies, thoughts, and ideas, and while you may choose to share your dreams with others, this choice should always remain yours. Keeping your journal in a drawer beside your bed is perhaps best; you need to have easy access to it when you wake up from a dream.

2. If you don't remember your dreams, begin by writing down your daydreams. Every one of us dreams; science has shown that dreaming occurs during Rapid Eye Movement (REM), the second stage of sleep. Yet while we all dream, not all of us remember our dreams. Write down your daydreams until you begin to recall your night dreams. Daydreams can say a lot about who you are, too.

3. Review your dreams. Every now and again, look over your dream journal to see what themes have been unfolding. You will soon notice how your dreams are affected by your external environment, and you will learn a lot about yourself through a better understanding of how you view the symbols in your dreams. While some symbols may have universal meaning, it is your unique interpretation of a symbol that will help you uncover a dream's message. This doesn't mean that universal symbolic meaning doesn't have its place—many of us identify strongly with the archetypal meanings of a symbol—for example, water as emotion. What I would like to make clear is that your interpretations of a symbol are just as important, so don't censor any associations you may have with a symbol simply because you think it sounds too far-fetched.

4. I've said it before, and I'll probably say it again: Don't be too concerned with trying to express your dream exactly in the way you experienced it in the dream state. Writing down your dreams is an enjoyable exercise, not a tedious one. Anyway, it's impossible to perfectly recapture your dream, because you are no longer the person *having* the dream, but the person *writing* about it. These are two distinct experiences. Yet, having said that, there are a few things you can do to make the record of your dream relate better to the actual experience. First, write in the present tense; second, draw your dream symbols; and third, express your dream feelings. These simple suggestions will bring you closer to the dream experience.

5. Write your dreams down as soon as you wake up. Don't tell yourself you'll do it later. You'll find that even if you allow a short time to pass, the memory of your dream will fade away. At first, writing down your dreams may require more effort because you are fighting against habit. We all like to stay in the familiar, so don't let uncomfortable feelings stop you from forging ahead.

6. Ask yourself questions about your dream. In addition to asking yourself the key questions I suggest, get into the habit of asking as many questions as you can concerning the dream. If you dream you were on a plane, ask yourself why you were on a plane. Similarly, if you dream you were in a foreign country, ask yourself what that country signifies to you. Also, if people you know appear in your dream, ask yourself how you feel about them and what they represent to you. Have you been spending a lot of time with them recently? Are they members of your family? What is your relationship like with them? The more questions you ask, the closer you come to the dream. Some answers won't come spontaneously, so sit with them. Don't worry about trying to immediately understand your dream. While some dreams will seem straightforward, you may be completely baffled by others. Be patient. Vital clues may come with dreams that follow.

7. Don't try to package each dream into a neatly summarized exposition. Dreams, like life, don't come in neat packages.

As much as you might like order in your life, there will always be elements of disorder and imperfection. It's the same with your dream journal. Working with it may heighten your intuition and self-awareness, but don't expect it to perfectly order your thoughts and feelings. Like anything that challenges you, there will be moments of frustration. Sometimes the meaning of a dream will completely elude you. This is part of the whole process, and a necessary one at that.

8. After you've become familiar with your dream journal, try this method of dream interpretation. Get yourself a blank piece of paper, and at the top, write: *This dream is telling me . . .* This is a great way to express your associations with the dream. Remember to write whatever comes to mind. Don't censor it or try to make sense of it; just write. Then, put it away. A couple of days later, reread it. You may be surprised at your insight.

9. Pay attention to the action in your dream. Think about how you were acting and how others were acting toward you. Were you running from someone?

Were you trying to tell someone something to no avail? Was someone doing something to you? What are your feelings about what was happening? You can use this information to bring about personal change in your life. Perhaps something in your dream made you feel uncomfortable, awkward, or downright awful. Try rewriting the reaction. For example, if you dreamed that you were running away from someone, rewrite it so that instead of running, you turned to confront the person. What happens? When you do this, you are consciously recognizing that you would like to change something about yourself, and, as you know, change *does* come with self-awareness.

10. Write an ending to your unfinished dreams. You know the type—you are just about to kiss the man/woman of your dreams when suddenly you wake up; you are just about to take the plunge of a lifetime when the phone rings; or perhaps you keep waking yourself from a nightmare that you want to see through to the end. Next time you do wake up from a dream you would have liked to have seen through to the end, write it down. Then keep on writing, creating your own ending. Make sure you keep the dream record separate from the ending you devise, because later on you may have a similar dream that *does* have an ending that you can compare to the one you wrote while awake.

There are hundreds of ways in which you can utilize a dream journal. The suggestions presented here are but a tiny sample. You will discover your own unique and enjoyable ways to use your dream journal as your inner journey unfolds.

When taking your first tentative steps, a dream dictionary may be helpful. My book *Interpreting Dreams A-Z* was created as a companion to this dream journal. Its focus is on assisting the individual to interpret and understand their own dreams. The A-Z of symbol meanings can be used as a diving board. I've made it clear that these meanings are not definitive, but are there to spark the reader's own imagination. Also included are questions for the dreamer to consider in relation to the symbols that appear in their dreams. Again, these questions are only there as a kick-start. The idea is to encourage you to ask your own questions, and to have fun!

Whether you feel a dream dictionary may be helpful or not, remember that this is your own unique journey. The idea is for you to begin interpreting your dreams in a way that individually suits you. As a dream coach, I wish you all the best on your journey.

Go for it!

How to Use Your Dream Journal

I remember a friend approaching me after she had started her dream journal, and saying, "I'm writing down my dreams—what next?"

It was this question that prompted me to create a dream journal with a difference. Rather than present readers with a journal of blank pages and quotes, I realized that it would be more useful to include essential questions and tips to guide the reader toward interpreting their own dreams.

You will find that this journal is designed to help you better understand your dreams in relation to your waking life. This, in turn, will help you integrate the two. It offers you all the tools necessary to interpret your dreams alone. Once you become accustomed to looking at your dreams in this format, dream interpretation will become second nature, and over time you will discover more techniques to assist you. Listening to and working with your dreams is a journey of ever-increasing depth.

When you record a dream, just follow the steps I've detailed below.

1. As soon as you wake up from a dream, pick up your dream journal, fill in the date, and give your dream a title. A title sums up the dream and helps you to recall its contents.

2. Fill in the Dream Scape, drawing the major symbols that appeared in your dream in the space provided. Like painting a landscape, you fill in the major symbols first, then begin to add detail. Drawing the symbols will help you discover more about their individual meanings within your dream—that is, a drawing can say more than a single word. Drawing the dream symbol allows you to create from the right brain, while simultaneously using the left, analytical brain to bring greater clarity. In this way, you are not just relying on the left brain to interpret your dreams, but integrating both the creative and the analytical. The drawings don't have to be masterpieces, just adequate representations. If you really don't like to draw, you can make a collage, using magazines to find and cut out appropriate pictures.

3. Once you have designated the important dream symbols, note whether your dream is recurring. Dreams recur for a reason: They contain important themes, and they deserve special attention.

4. Record the central dream motif. The dream motif is the predominant theme, action, or situation that occurs during your dream. For example, you may have dreamed about all the members of your family—if so, the motif would be "family." Location may also be an important motif.

5. Now write down your dream, using the present tense. Don't be restricted by the space provided. If you need more room, continue the record in a bound notebook, remembering to date the dream and give it the appropriate heading. Once you have written out your dream, use a highlighter to accent the important symbols or themes.

6. Briefly fill in the section called "About You." It may take you some time to recognize just how important these questions can be in helping you interpret your dream. A friend has been recording her dreams in this way for a few months now, and only recently discovered an important pattern: Her diet was affect-

ing her dreams. Over time, you too will recognize important links between your everyday life and your dreams.

7. Next, write down your conclusion. What do you think your dream was about? It isn't necessary to fill this out immediately. You may not fully understand a dream for a couple of days—maybe even a couple of weeks. Also, you may redefine your conclusion after subsequent dreams provide you with greater clarity.

8. Finally, go back to the front of the form and fill in the "Quote" section with a statement or affirmation that seems to sum up the overall feeling of the dream. As you fill in the days of your dream journal, you will be able to quickly flip through the pages and scan these quotes in order to determine any recurring themes.

The most important aspect of dream recording is to make it part of your everyday life. If you regularly record your dreams and consider their meanings, you will become well versed in your own unique language of symbols and meanings, and you will learn to use them to take a fresh approach to your everyday life.

EDITOR'S NOTE: You may wish to copy one of the blank forms so you will always have a supply on hand.

SAMPLE DREAM: I have included one sample spread to help you get the feel for using this dream journal. If the dream intrigues you, as a fun exercise, rework what I have done. You will be amazed at how different the conclusions can be even though the same dream is being interpreted.

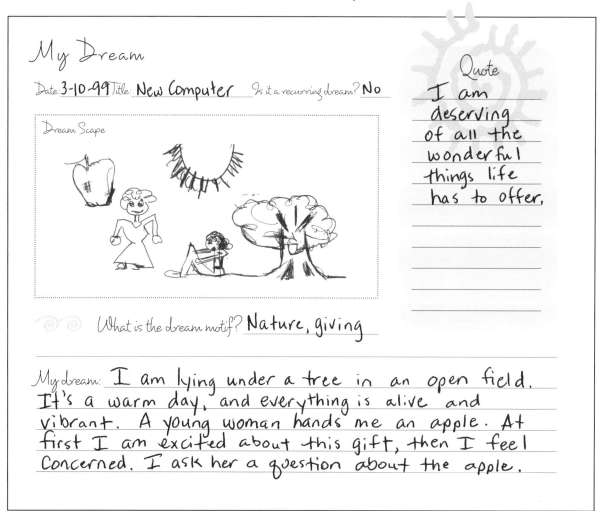

My Dream

Date: 3-10-99 Title: New Computer Is it a recurring dream? No

Dream Scape

Quote
I am deserving of all the wonderful things life has to offer.

What is the dream motif? Nature, giving

My dream: I am lying under a tree in an open field. It's a warm day, and everything is alive and vibrant. A young woman hands me an apple. At first I am excited about this gift, then I feel concerned. I ask her a question about the apple.

Relief washes over me when she answers the question, and I feel joy again at receiving this gift. (I don't remember the question I asked her.)

About You

What time did you go to bed? **around midnight**

What did you eat before going to bed? **biscuits**

What did you watch, read, or listen to? **TV, sports**

What kind of mood were you in? **apprehensive**

What did you drink? **tea**

Did you take any medication? **no**

What was your focus at the moment?

Relationship_____ Travel_____ Career **X** Abundance_____

Health_____ Other_____

My Conclusion

The tree and the scenery represent nature and relaxation — something I would like to enjoy more of. The apple symbolizes a computer (Apple Mac). the question concerned purchasing one or not: should I upgrade, can I afford it, do I have the expertise to use it? The young woman's answer reinforced my decision to buy it.

My Dream

Date:_____ Title:_____ Is it a recurring dream?_____

Dream Scape

_____
_____
_____
_____
_____
_____
_____
_____
_____
_____
_____

What is the dream motif? _____

My dream:_____

_____

_____

_____

_____

My Dream, cont'd.

_____
_____
_____
_____

About You

What time did you go to bed? _____

What did you eat before going to bed? _____

What did you watch, read, or listen to? _____

What kind of mood were you in? _____

What did you drink? _____

Did you take any medication? _____

What was your focus at the moment?

Relationship_____ Travel_____ Career_____ Abundance_____

Health_____ Other_____

My Conclusion

_____
_____
_____
_____
_____
_____
_____
_____
_____
_____
_____
_____

My Dream

Date:_____ Title:_____ Is it a recurring dream?_____

Dream Scape

_____

_____

_____

_____

_____

_____

_____

_____

_____

_____

What is the dream motif?_____

_____

My dream:_____

_____

_____

_____

_____

My Dream, cont'd.

_____
_____
_____
_____

About You

What time did you go to bed? _____

What did you eat before going to bed? _____

What did you watch, read, or listen to? _____

What kind of mood were you in? _____

What did you drink? _____

Did you take any medication? _____

What was your focus at the moment?

Relationship____ Travel____ Career____ Abundance____

Health____ Other____

My Conclusion

_____
_____
_____
_____
_____
_____
_____
_____
_____
_____

My Dream

Date: _____ Title: _____ Is it a recurring dream? _____

Dream Scape

_____

_____

_____

_____

_____

_____

_____

_____

_____

_____

_____

What is the dream motif? _____

_____

My dream: _____

_____

_____

_____

_____

_____

_____

_____

_____

About You

What time did you go to bed? _____

What did you eat before going to bed? _____

What did you watch, read, or listen to? _____

What kind of mood were you in? _____

What did you drink? _____

Did you take any medication? _____

What was your focus at the moment?

Relationship_____ Travel_____ Career_____ Abundance_____

Health_____ Other_____

My Conclusion

_____

_____

_____

_____

_____

_____

_____

_____

_____

_____

_____

_____

My Dream

Date: _____ Title: _____ Is it a recurring dream? _____

Dream Scape

What is the dream motif? _____

_____

My dream: _____

_____

_____

_____

_____

Quote

_____

_____

_____

_____

_____

_____

_____

_____

_____

_____

_____

_____

_____

_____

_____

About You

What time did you go to bed? _____

What did you eat before going to bed? _____

What did you watch, read, or listen to? _____

What kind of mood were you in? _____

What did you drink? _____

Did you take any medication? _____

What was your focus at the moment?

Relationship_____ Travel_____ Career_____ Abundance_____

Health_____ Other_____

My Conclusion

_____

_____

_____

_____

_____

_____

_____

_____

_____

_____

_____

_____

_____

My Dream

Date:_____ Title:_____ Is it a recurring dream?_____

Dream Scape

What is the dream motif?_____

_____

My dream:_____

_____

_____

_____

_____

_____

_____

_____

_____

About You

My Conclusion

What time did you go to bed? _____

What did you eat before going to bed? _____

What did you watch, read, or listen to? _____

What kind of mood were you in? _____

What did you drink? _____

Did you take any medication? _____

What was your focus at the moment?

Relationship_____ Travel_____ Career_____ Abundance_____

Health_____ Other_____

_____

_____

_____

_____

_____

_____

_____

_____

_____

_____

_____

My Dream

Date:_____ Title:_____ Is it a recurring dream?_____

Dream Scape

What is the dream motif?_____

My dream:_____
_____
_____
_____
_____

My Dream, cont'd.

_____
_____
_____
_____

About You

What time did you go to bed? _____

What did you eat before going to bed? _____

What did you watch, read, or listen to? _____

What kind of mood were you in? _____

What did you drink? _____

Did you take any medication? _____

What was your focus at the moment?

Relationship_____ Travel_____ Career_____ Abundance_____

Health_____ Other_____

My Conclusion

_____
_____
_____
_____
_____
_____
_____
_____
_____
_____
_____
_____
_____
_____

My Dream

Date: _____ Title: _____ Is it a recurring dream? _____

Dream Scape

_____
_____
_____
_____
_____
_____
_____
_____
_____
_____
_____

What is the dream motif? _____

My dream: _____
_____
_____
_____
_____

My Dream, cont'd.

_____
_____
_____
_____

About You

What time did you go to bed? _____

What did you eat before going to bed? _____

What did you watch, read, or listen to? _____

What kind of mood were you in? _____

What did you drink? _____

Did you take any medication? _____

What was your focus at the moment?

Relationship_____ Travel_____ Career_____ Abundance_____

Health_____ Other_____

My Conclusion

_____
_____
_____
_____
_____
_____
_____
_____
_____
_____
_____
_____
_____
_____

My Dream

Date:_____ Title:_____ Is it a recurring dream?_____

Dream Scape

What is the dream motif?_____

My dream:_____
_____
_____
_____
_____

My Dream, cont'd.

_____
_____
_____
_____
_____

About You

What time did you go to bed? _____

What did you eat before going to bed? _____

What did you watch, read, or listen to? _____

What kind of mood were you in? _____

What did you drink? _____

Did you take any medication? _____

What was your focus at the moment?

Relationship____ Travel____ Career____ Abundance____

Health____ Other____

My Conclusion

_____
_____
_____
_____
_____
_____
_____
_____
_____
_____
_____
_____

My Dream

Date:_____ Title:_____ Is it a recurring dream?_____

Dream Scape

What is the dream motif?_____

My dream:_____

_____

_____

_____

_____

About You

My Conclusion

What time did you go to bed? _____

What did you eat before going to bed? _____

What did you watch, read, or listen to? _____

What kind of mood were you in? _____

What did you drink? _____

Did you take any medication? _____

What was your focus at the moment?

Relationship_____Travel_____Career_____Abundance_____

Health_____Other_____

_____

_____

_____

_____

_____

_____

_____

_____

_____

_____

_____

_____

_____

_____

My Dream

Date:_____ Title:_____ Is it a recurring dream?_____

Dream Scape

What is the dream motif?_____

_____

My dream:_____

_____

_____

_____

_____

_____
_____
_____
_____

About You

What time did you go to bed? _____

What did you eat before going to bed? _____

What did you watch, read, or listen to? _____

What kind of mood were you in? _____

What did you drink? _____

Did you take any medication? _____

What was your focus at the moment?

Relationship_____ Travel_____ Career_____ Abundance_____

Health_____ Other_____

My Conclusion

_____
_____
_____
_____
_____
_____
_____
_____
_____
_____
_____
_____
_____

My Dream

Date:_____ Title:_____ Is it a recurring dream?_____

Dream Scape

What is the dream motif?_____

_____

My dream:_____

_____

_____

_____

_____

_____

_____

_____

_____

_____

_____

_____

_____

_____

_____

My Dream, cont'd.

_____
_____
_____
_____

About You

What time did you go to bed? _____

What did you eat before going to bed? _____

What did you watch, read, or listen to? _____

What kind of mood were you in? _____

What did you drink? _____

Did you take any medication? _____

What was your focus at the moment?

Relationship_____ Travel_____ Career_____ Abundance_____

Health_____ Other_____

My Conclusion

_____
_____
_____
_____
_____
_____
_____
_____
_____
_____
_____

My Dream

Date:_____ Title:_____ Is it a recurring dream?_____

Dream Scape

What is the dream motif?_____

My dream:_____

My Dream, cont'd.

_____
_____
_____
_____

About You

What time did you go to bed? _____

What did you eat before going to bed? _____

What did you watch, read, or listen to? _____

What kind of mood were you in? _____

What did you drink? _____

Did you take any medication? _____

What was your focus at the moment?

Relationship_____ Travel_____ Career_____ Abundance_____

Health_____ Other_____

My Conclusion

_____
_____
_____
_____
_____
_____
_____
_____
_____
_____
_____
_____

My Dream

Date:_____ Title:_____ Is it a recurring dream?_____

Dream Scape

_____
_____
_____
_____
_____
_____
_____
_____
_____
_____
_____

What is the dream motif?_____

My dream:_____
_____
_____
_____
_____

_____
_____
_____
_____

About You

My Conclusion

What time did you go to bed? _____

What did you eat before going to bed? _____

What did you watch, read, or listen to? _____

What kind of mood were you in? _____

What did you drink? _____

Did you take any medication? _____

What was your focus at the moment?

Relationship_____ Travel_____ Career_____ Abundance_____

Health_____ Other_____

_____
_____
_____
_____
_____
_____
_____
_____
_____
_____
_____
_____
_____

My Dream

Date:_____ Title:_____ Is it a recurring dream? _____

Dream Scape

_____
_____
_____
_____
_____
_____
_____
_____
_____
_____

What is the dream motif?_____

_____

My dream:_____

_____

_____

_____

My Dream, cont'd.

_____
_____
_____
_____
_____

About You

What time did you go to bed? _____

What did you eat before going to bed? _____

What did you watch, read, or listen to? _____

What kind of mood were you in? _____

What did you drink? _____

Did you take any medication? _____

What was your focus at the moment?

Relationship_____ Travel_____ Career_____ Abundance_____

Health_____ Other_____

My Conclusion

_____
_____
_____
_____
_____
_____
_____
_____
_____
_____
_____
_____

My Dream

Date: _____ Title: _____ Is it a recurring dream? _____

Dream Scape

What is the dream motif? _____

_____

My dream: _____

_____

_____

_____

_____

Quote

_____
_____
_____
_____
_____
_____
_____
_____
_____
_____

_____
_____
_____
_____

About You

What time did you go to bed? _____

What did you eat before going to bed? _____

What did you watch, read, or listen to? _____

What kind of mood were you in? _____

What did you drink? _____

Did you take any medication? _____

What was your focus at the moment?

Relationship_____ Travel_____ Career_____ Abundance_____

Health_____ Other_____

My Conclusion

_____
_____
_____
_____
_____
_____
_____
_____
_____
_____
_____
_____
_____

My Dream

Date: _____ Title: _____ Is it a recurring dream? _____

_____

_____

_____

_____

_____

_____

_____

_____

_____

Dream Scape

What is the dream motif? _____

My dream: _____

_____

_____

_____

_____

_____
_____
_____
_____

About You

What time did you go to bed? _____

What did you eat before going to bed? _____

What did you watch, read, or listen to? _____

What kind of mood were you in? _____

What did you drink? _____

Did you take any medication? _____

What was your focus at the moment?

Relationship____ Travel____ Career____ Abundance____

Health____ Other____

My Conclusion

_____
_____
_____
_____
_____
_____
_____
_____
_____
_____
_____
_____

My Dream

Date:_____ Title:_____ Is it a recurring dream?_____

Dream Scape

What is the dream motif?_____

My dream:_____
_____
_____
_____
_____

My Dream, cont'd.

_____
_____
_____
_____
_____

About You

What time did you go to bed? _____

What did you eat before going to bed? _____

What did you watch, read, or listen to? _____

What kind of mood were you in? _____

What did you drink? _____

Did you take any medication? _____

What was your focus at the moment?

Relationship_____ Travel_____ Career_____ Abundance_____

Health_____ Other_____

My Conclusion

_____
_____
_____
_____
_____
_____
_____
_____
_____
_____
_____

My Dream

Date: _____ Title: _____ Is it a recurring dream? _____

Dream Scape

What is the dream motif? _____

My dream: _____

_____
_____
_____
_____

About You

What time did you go to bed? _____

What did you eat before going to bed? _____

What did you watch, read, or listen to? _____

What kind of mood were you in? _____

What did you drink? _____

Did you take any medication? _____

What was your focus at the moment?

Relationship _____ Travel _____ Career _____ Abundance _____

Health _____ Other _____

My Conclusion

_____
_____
_____
_____
_____
_____
_____
_____
_____
_____
_____
_____

My Dream

Date: _____ Title: _____ Is it a recurring dream? _____

Dream Scape

_____

_____

_____

_____

_____

_____

_____

_____

_____

_____

What is the dream motif? _____

My dream: _____

_____

_____

_____

_____

About You

What time did you go to bed? _____

What did you eat before going to bed? _____

What did you watch, read, or listen to? _____

What kind of mood were you in? _____

What did you drink? _____

Did you take any medication? _____

What was your focus at the moment?

Relationship_____ Travel_____ Career_____ Abundance_____

Health_____ Other_____

My Conclusion

_____

_____

_____

_____

_____

_____

_____

_____

_____

_____

_____

_____

My Dream

Date:_____ Title:_____ Is it a recurring dream?_____

Dream Scape

What is the dream motif?_____

My dream:_____
_____
_____
_____
_____

Quote
_____
_____
_____
_____
_____
_____
_____
_____
_____
_____

_____
_____
_____
_____

About You

What time did you go to bed? _____

What did you eat before going to bed? _____

What did you watch, read, or listen to? _____

What kind of mood were you in? _____

What did you drink? _____

Did you take any medication? _____

What was your focus at the moment?

Relationship_____ Travel_____ Career_____ Abundance_____

Health_____ Other_____

My Conclusion

_____
_____
_____
_____
_____
_____
_____
_____
_____
_____
_____
_____
_____

My Dream

Date:_____ Title:_____ Is it a recurring dream?_____

Dream Scape

What is the dream motif?_____

My dream:_____

_____

_____

_____

_____

_____

_____

_____

_____

About You

What time did you go to bed? _____

What did you eat before going to bed? _____

What did you watch, read, or listen to? _____

What kind of mood were you in? _____

What did you drink? _____

Did you take any medication? _____

What was your focus at the moment?

Relationship_____ Travel_____ Career_____ Abundance_____

Health_____ Other_____

My Conclusion

_____

_____

_____

_____

_____

_____

_____

_____

_____

_____

_____

_____

My Dream

Date:_____ Title:_____ Is it a recurring dream?_____

Dream Scape

_____

What is the dream motif?_____

My dream:_____

_____

_____

_____

_____

_____

_____

_____

_____

About You

What time did you go to bed? _____

What did you eat before going to bed? _____

What did you watch, read, or listen to? _____

What kind of mood were you in? _____

What did you drink? _____

Did you take any medication? _____

What was your focus at the moment?

Relationship____ Travel____ Career____ Abundance____

Health____ Other____

My Conclusion

_____

_____

_____

_____

_____

_____

_____

_____

_____

_____

_____

_____

_____

My Dream

Date:_____ Title:_____ Is it a recurring dream?_____

Dream Scape

What is the dream motif?_____

My dream:_____

_____

_____

_____

_____

About You

My Conclusion

What time did you go to bed? _____

What did you eat before going to bed? _____

What did you watch, read, or listen to? _____

What kind of mood were you in? _____

What did you drink? _____

Did you take any medication? _____

What was your focus at the moment?

Relationship_____ Travel_____ Career_____ Abundance_____

Health_____ Other_____

_____

_____

_____

_____

_____

_____

_____

_____

_____

_____

_____

My Dream

Date:_____ Title:_____ Is it a recurring dream?_____

Dream Scape

What is the dream motif?_____

_____

My dream:_____

_____
_____
_____
_____
_____

_____
_____
_____
_____

About You

My Conclusion

What time did you go to bed? _____

What did you eat before going to bed? _____

What did you watch, read, or listen to? _____

What kind of mood were you in? _____

What did you drink? _____

Did you take any medication? _____

What was your focus at the moment?

Relationship_____ Travel_____ Career_____ Abundance_____

Health_____ Other_____

_____
_____
_____
_____
_____
_____
_____
_____
_____
_____
_____
_____

My Dream

Date:_____ Title:_____ Is it a recurring dream?_____

Dream Scape

What is the dream motif?_____

My dream:_____

_____

_____

_____

_____

Quote

_____

_____

_____

_____

_____

_____

_____

_____

_____

_____

_____

_____

_____

_____

_____

About You

What time did you go to bed? _____

What did you eat before going to bed? _____

What did you watch, read, or listen to? _____

What kind of mood were you in? _____

What did you drink? _____

Did you take any medication? _____

What was your focus at the moment?

Relationship_____ Travel_____ Career_____ Abundance_____

Health_____ Other_____

My Conclusion

_____

_____

_____

_____

_____

_____

_____

_____

_____

_____

_____

My Dream

Date:_____ Title:_____ Is it a recurring dream?_____

Dream Scape

What is the dream motif?_____

My dream:_____

_____

_____

_____

_____

My Dream, cont'd.

_____

_____

_____

_____

About You

What time did you go to bed? _____

What did you eat before going to bed? _____

What did you watch, read, or listen to? _____

What kind of mood were you in? _____

What did you drink? _____

Did you take any medication? _____

What was your focus at the moment?

Relationship____ Travel____ Career____ Abundance____

Health____ Other____

My Conclusion

_____

_____

_____

_____

_____

_____

_____

_____

_____

_____

_____

My Dream

Date: _____ Title: _____ Is it a recurring dream? _____

Dream Scape

What is the dream motif? _____

My dream: _____

_____

_____

_____

_____

About You

My Conclusion

What time did you go to bed? _____

What did you eat before going to bed? _____

What did you watch, read, or listen to? _____

What kind of mood were you in? _____

What did you drink? _____

Did you take any medication? _____

What was your focus at the moment?

Relationship ____ Travel ____ Career ____ Abundance ____

Health ____ Other ____

_____

_____

_____

_____

_____

_____

_____

_____

_____

_____

_____

My Dream

Date:_____ Title:_____ Is it a recurring dream?_____

Dream Scape

What is the dream motif?_____

My dream:_____

_____

_____

_____

_____

_____

_____

_____

_____

About You

What time did you go to bed? _____

What did you eat before going to bed? _____

What did you watch, read, or listen to? _____

What kind of mood were you in? _____

What did you drink? _____

Did you take any medication? _____

What was your focus at the moment?

Relationship____ Travel____ Career____ Abundance____

Health____ Other____

My Conclusion

_____

_____

_____

_____

_____

_____

_____

_____

_____

_____

_____

_____

My Dream

Date:_____ Title:_____ Is it a recurring dream?_____

```
Dream Scape
```

What is the dream motif?_____

My dream:_____
_____
_____
_____
_____

My Dream, cont'd.

_____
_____
_____
_____

About You

What time did you go to bed? _____

What did you eat before going to bed? _____

What did you watch, read, or listen to? _____

What kind of mood were you in? _____

What did you drink? _____

Did you take any medication? _____

What was your focus at the moment?

Relationship_____ Travel_____ Career_____ Abundance_____

Health_____ Other_____

My Conclusion

_____
_____
_____
_____
_____
_____
_____
_____
_____
_____
_____
_____

My Dream

Date:_____ Title:_____ Is it a recurring dream?_____

Dream Scape

What is the dream motif?_____

My dream:_____

_____

_____

_____

_____

Quote

_____

_____

_____

_____

_____

_____

_____

_____

_____

_____

_____

My Dream, cont'd.

_____
_____
_____
_____

About You

What time did you go to bed? _____

What did you eat before going to bed? _____

What did you watch, read, or listen to? _____

What kind of mood were you in? _____

What did you drink? _____

Did you take any medication? _____

What was your focus at the moment?

Relationship____ Travel____ Career____ Abundance____

Health____ Other____

My Conclusion

_____
_____
_____
_____
_____
_____
_____
_____
_____
_____
_____
_____
_____

My Dream

Date:_____ Title:_____ Is it a recurring dream?_____

Dream Scape

_____
_____
_____
_____
_____
_____
_____
_____
_____
_____

What is the dream motif?_____

My dream:_____
_____
_____
_____
_____

My Dream, cont'd.

_____
_____
_____
_____
_____

About You

My Conclusion

What time did you go to bed? _____

What did you eat before going to bed? _____

What did you watch, read, or listen to? _____

What kind of mood were you in? _____

What did you drink? _____

Did you take any medication? _____

What was your focus at the moment?

Relationship____ Travel____ Career____ Abundance____

Health____ Other____

_____
_____
_____
_____
_____
_____
_____
_____
_____
_____
_____
_____

My Dream

Date:_____ Title:_____ Is it a recurring dream?_____

Dream Scape

What is the dream motif?_____

My dream:_____

My Dream, cont'd.

_____
_____
_____
_____

About You

What time did you go to bed? _____

What did you eat before going to bed? _____

What did you watch, read, or listen to? _____

What kind of mood were you in? _____

What did you drink? _____

Did you take any medication? _____

What was your focus at the moment?

Relationship_____ Travel_____ Career_____ Abundance_____

Health_____ Other_____

My Conclusion

_____
_____
_____
_____
_____
_____
_____
_____
_____
_____
_____
_____

My Dream

Date:_____ Title:_____ Is it a recurring dream?_____

Dream Scape

_____
_____
_____
_____
_____
_____
_____
_____
_____
_____
_____

What is the dream motif?_____

_____

My dream:_____

_____
_____
_____
_____

_____

_____

_____

_____

About You

What time did you go to bed? _____

What did you eat before going to bed? _____

What did you watch, read, or listen to? _____

What kind of mood were you in? _____

What did you drink? _____

Did you take any medication? _____

What was your focus at the moment?

Relationship_____ Travel_____ Career_____ Abundance_____

Health_____ Other_____

My Conclusion

_____

_____

_____

_____

_____

_____

_____

_____

_____

_____

_____

_____

My Dream

Date:_____ Title:_____ Is it a recurring dream?_____

Dream Scape

_____
_____
_____
_____
_____
_____
_____
_____
_____
_____

What is the dream motif?_____

My dream:_____
_____
_____
_____
_____

My Dream, cont'd.

_____
_____
_____
_____
_____

About You

What time did you go to bed? _____

What did you eat before going to bed? _____

What did you watch, read, or listen to? _____

What kind of mood were you in? _____

What did you drink? _____

Did you take any medication? _____

What was your focus at the moment?

Relationship____ Travel____ Career____ Abundance____

Health____ Other____

My Conclusion

_____
_____
_____
_____
_____
_____
_____
_____
_____
_____
_____
_____

My Dream

Date: _____ Title: _____ Is it a recurring dream? _____

Dream Scape

What is the dream motif? _____

_____

My dream: _____

_____

_____

_____

_____

_____

_____

_____

_____

About You

What time did you go to bed? _____

What did you eat before going to bed? _____

What did you watch, read, or listen to? _____

What kind of mood were you in? _____

What did you drink? _____

Did you take any medication? _____

What was your focus at the moment?

Relationship_____ Travel_____ Career_____ Abundance_____

Health_____ Other_____

My Conclusion

_____

_____

_____

_____

_____

_____

_____

_____

_____

_____

_____

_____

My Dream

Date:_____ Title:_____ Is it a recurring dream?_____

Dream Scape

What is the dream motif?_____

_____

My dream:_____

_____

_____

_____

_____

Quote

_____

_____

_____

_____

_____

_____

_____

_____

_____

_____

_____

My Dream, cont'd.

_____
_____
_____
_____

About You

What time did you go to bed?_____

What did you eat before going to bed?_____

What did you watch, read, or listen to?_____

What kind of mood were you in?_____

What did you drink?_____

Did you take any medication?_____

What was your focus at the moment?

Relationship____ Travel____ Career____ Abundance____

Health____ Other____

My Conclusion

_____
_____
_____
_____
_____
_____
_____
_____
_____
_____
_____
_____
_____

My Dream

Date:_____ Title:_____ Is it a recurring dream?_____

Dream Scape

_____
_____
_____
_____
_____
_____
_____
_____
_____
_____

What is the dream motif?_____

My dream:_____

_____

_____

_____

_____

_____
_____
_____
_____

About You

What time did you go to bed? _____

What did you eat before going to bed? _____

What did you watch, read, or listen to? _____

What kind of mood were you in? _____

What did you drink? _____

Did you take any medication? _____

What was your focus at the moment?

Relationship_____ Travel_____ Career_____ Abundance_____

Health_____ Other_____

My Conclusion

_____
_____
_____
_____
_____
_____
_____
_____
_____
_____
_____
_____

My Dream

Date:_____ Title:_____ Is it a recurring dream? _____

Dream Scape

Quote
_____
_____
_____
_____
_____
_____
_____
_____
_____
_____
_____

What is the dream motif?_____

_____

My dream:_____

_____

_____

_____

_____

My Dream, cont'd.

_____

_____

_____

_____

About You

What time did you go to bed? _____

What did you eat before going to bed? _____

What did you watch, read, or listen to? _____

What kind of mood were you in? _____

What did you drink? _____

Did you take any medication? _____

What was your focus at the moment?

Relationship_____ Travel_____ Career_____ Abundance_____

Health_____ Other_____

My Conclusion

_____

_____

_____

_____

_____

_____

_____

_____

_____

_____

_____

_____

My Dream

Date:_____ Title:_____ Is it a recurring dream?_____

Dream Scape

What is the dream motif?_____

My dream:_____

_____
_____
_____
_____

About You

What time did you go to bed? _____

What did you eat before going to bed? _____

What did you watch, read, or listen to? _____

What kind of mood were you in? _____

What did you drink? _____

Did you take any medication? _____

What was your focus at the moment?

Relationship_____Travel_____Career_____Abundance_____

Health_____Other_____

My Conclusion

_____
_____
_____
_____
_____
_____
_____
_____
_____
_____
_____
_____

My Dream

Date:_____ Title:_____ Is it a recurring dream? _____

Quote
_____
_____
_____
_____
_____
_____
_____
_____
_____
_____
_____
_____

Dream Scape

What is the dream motif? _____

_____

My dream: _____
_____
_____
_____
_____

My Dream, cont'd.

_____
_____
_____
_____

About You

What time did you go to bed? _____

What did you eat before going to bed? _____

What did you watch, read, or listen to? _____

What kind of mood were you in? _____

What did you drink? _____

Did you take any medication? _____

What was your focus at the moment?

Relationship_____ Travel_____ Career_____ Abundance_____

Health_____ Other_____

My Conclusion

_____
_____
_____
_____
_____
_____
_____
_____
_____
_____
_____
_____
_____

My Dream

Date:_____ Title:_____Is it a recurring dream?_____

Dream Scape

_____
_____
_____
_____
_____
_____
_____
_____
_____
_____

What is the dream motif?_____

My dream:_____
_____
_____
_____
_____

_____
_____
_____
_____

About You

What time did you go to bed? _____

What did you eat before going to bed? _____

What did you watch, read, or listen to? _____

What kind of mood were you in? _____

What did you drink? _____

Did you take any medication? _____

What was your focus at the moment?

Relationship_____ Travel_____ Career_____ Abundance_____

Health_____ Other_____

My Conclusion

_____
_____
_____
_____
_____
_____
_____
_____
_____
_____
_____

My Dream

Date: _____ Title: _____ Is it a recurring dream? _____

Dream Scape

_____
_____
_____
_____
_____
_____
_____
_____
_____
_____
_____

What is the dream motif? _____

My dream: _____
_____
_____
_____
_____

_____
_____
_____
_____
_____

About You

What time did you go to bed? _____

What did you eat before going to bed? _____

What did you watch, read, or listen to? _____

What kind of mood were you in? _____

What did you drink? _____

Did you take any medication? _____

What was your focus at the moment?

Relationship_____ Travel_____ Career_____ Abundance_____

Health_____ Other_____

My Conclusion

_____
_____
_____
_____
_____
_____
_____
_____
_____
_____
_____

My Dream

Date:_____ Title:_____ Is it a recurring dream?_____

Dream Scape

What is the dream motif?_____

My dream:_____

_____

_____

_____

_____

Quote

_____
_____
_____
_____
_____
_____
_____
_____
_____
_____
_____

_____
_____
_____
_____

About You

What time did you go to bed? _____

What did you eat before going to bed? _____

What did you watch, read, or listen to? _____

What kind of mood were you in? _____

What did you drink? _____

Did you take any medication? _____

What was your focus at the moment?

Relationship_____ Travel_____ Career_____ Abundance_____

Health_____ Other_____

My Conclusion

_____
_____
_____
_____
_____
_____
_____
_____
_____
_____
_____

My Dream

Date: _____ Title: _____ Is it a recurring dream? _____

```
Dream Scape
```

ⓔⓔ ⓔ   What is the dream motif? _____

My dream: _____

_____

_____

_____

_____

My Dream, cont'd.

_____
_____
_____
_____

About You

What time did you go to bed? _____

What did you eat before going to bed? _____

What did you watch, read, or listen to? _____

What kind of mood were you in? _____

What did you drink? _____

Did you take any medication? _____

What was your focus at the moment?

Relationship_____ Travel_____ Career_____ Abundance_____

Health_____ Other_____

My Conclusion

_____
_____
_____
_____
_____
_____
_____
_____
_____
_____
_____
_____
_____

My Dream

Date: _____ Title: _____ Is it a recurring dream? _____

_____
_____
_____
_____
_____
_____
_____
_____
_____
_____

Dream Scape

What is the dream motif? _____

_____

My dream: _____
_____
_____
_____
_____

My Dream, cont'd.

_____
_____
_____
_____

About You

What time did you go to bed? _____

What did you eat before going to bed? _____

What did you watch, read, or listen to? _____

What kind of mood were you in? _____

What did you drink? _____

Did you take any medication? _____

What was your focus at the moment?

Relationship____ Travel____ Career____ Abundance____

Health____ Other____

My Conclusion

_____
_____
_____
_____
_____
_____
_____
_____
_____
_____
_____

My Dream

Date: _____ Title: _____ Is it a recurring dream? _____

```
.................................................................
: Dream Scape                                                   :
:                                                               :
:                                                               :
:                                                               :
:                                                               :
:                                                               :
:                                                               :
:                                                               :
:................................................................
```

What is the dream motif? _____

_____

My dream: _____

_____

_____

_____

_____

Quote

_____

_____

_____

_____

_____

_____

_____

_____

_____

_____

_____
_____
_____
_____

About You

What time did you go to bed? _____

What did you eat before going to bed? _____

What did you watch, read, or listen to? _____

What kind of mood were you in? _____

What did you drink? _____

Did you take any medication? _____

What was your focus at the moment?

Relationship_____Travel_____Career_____Abundance_____

Health_____Other_____

My Conclusion

_____
_____
_____
_____
_____
_____
_____
_____
_____
_____
_____
_____
_____

My Dream

Date:_____ Title:_____ Is it a recurring dream?_____

Dream Scape

What is the dream motif?_____

My dream:_____

_____

_____

_____

_____

Quote
_____
_____
_____
_____
_____
_____
_____
_____
_____
_____

_____
_____
_____
_____

About You

My Conclusion

What time did you go to bed? _____

What did you eat before going to bed? _____

What did you watch, read, or listen to? _____

What kind of mood were you in? _____

What did you drink? _____

Did you take any medication? _____

What was your focus at the moment?

Relationship_____ Travel_____ Career_____ Abundance_____

Health_____ Other_____

_____
_____
_____
_____
_____
_____
_____
_____
_____
_____
_____

My Dream

Date:_____ Title:_____ Is it a recurring dream?_____

Dream Scape

What is the dream motif?_____

My dream:_____

_____

_____

_____

_____

Quote

_____

_____

_____

_____

_____

_____

_____

_____

_____

_____

_____

_____

_____

_____

_____

◎ ◎ About You ◎ ◎

What time did you go to bed? _____

What did you eat before going to bed? _____

What did you watch, read, or listen to? _____

What kind of mood were you in? _____

What did you drink? _____

Did you take any medication? _____

What was your focus at the moment?

Relationship_____Travel_____Career_____Abundance_____

Health_____Other_____

My Conclusion

_____

_____

_____

_____

_____

_____

_____

_____

_____

_____

_____

_____

_____

My Dream

Date: _____ Title: _____ Is it a recurring dream? _____

Dream Scape

What is the dream motif? _____

My dream: _____
_____
_____
_____
_____

_____
_____
_____
_____

About You

My Conclusion

What time did you go to bed? _____

What did you eat before going to bed? _____

What did you watch, read, or listen to? _____

What kind of mood were you in? _____

What did you drink? _____

Did you take any medication? _____

What was your focus at the moment?

Relationship____ Travel____ Career____ Abundance____

Health____ Other____

_____
_____
_____
_____
_____
_____
_____
_____
_____
_____
_____
_____
_____
_____

My Dream

Date:_____ Title:_____ Is it a recurring dream?_____

Dream Scape

What is the dream motif?_____

_____

My dream:_____
_____
_____
_____
_____

Quote
_____
_____
_____
_____
_____
_____
_____
_____
_____
_____

_____

_____

_____

_____

About You

What time did you go to bed? _____

What did you eat before going to bed? _____

What did you watch, read, or listen to? _____

What kind of mood were you in? _____

What did you drink? _____

Did you take any medication? _____

What was your focus at the moment?

Relationship_____ Travel_____ Career_____ Abundance_____

Health_____ Other_____

My Conclusion

_____

_____

_____

_____

_____

_____

_____

_____

_____

_____

_____

My Dream

Date:_____ Title:_____ Is it a recurring dream?_____

Dream Scape

What is the dream motif?_____

My dream:_____
_____
_____
_____
_____

_____

_____

_____

_____

~ ~ About You ~ ~

What time did you go to bed? _____

What did you eat before going to bed? _____

What did you watch, read, or listen to? _____

What kind of mood were you in? _____

What did you drink? _____

Did you take any medication? _____

What was your focus at the moment?

Relationship_____ Travel_____ Career_____ Abundance_____

Health_____ Other_____

My Conclusion

_____

_____

_____

_____

_____

_____

_____

_____

_____

_____

_____

_____

My Dream

Date: _____ Title: _____ Is it a recurring dream? _____

Dream Scape

What is the dream motif? _____

My dream: _____

_____

_____

_____

_____

Quote

_____

_____

_____

_____

_____

_____

_____

_____

_____

_____

_____

My Dream, cont'd.

_____

_____

_____

_____

About You

What time did you go to bed? _____

What did you eat before going to bed? _____

What did you watch, read, or listen to? _____

What kind of mood were you in? _____

What did you drink? _____

Did you take any medication? _____

What was your focus at the moment?

Relationship_____ Travel_____ Career_____ Abundance_____

Health_____ Other_____

My Conclusion

_____

_____

_____

_____

_____

_____

_____

_____

_____

_____

_____

My Dream

Date: _____ Title: _____ Is it a recurring dream? _____

Quote
_____
_____
_____
_____
_____
_____
_____
_____
_____
_____
_____

Dream Scape

What is the dream motif? _____

My dream: _____
_____
_____
_____
_____

_____
_____
_____
_____

About You

My Conclusion

What time did you go to bed? _____

What did you eat before going to bed? _____

What did you watch, read, or listen to? _____

What kind of mood were you in? _____

What did you drink? _____

Did you take any medication? _____

What was your focus at the moment?

Relationship_____ Travel_____ Career_____ Abundance_____

Health_____ Other_____

_____
_____
_____
_____
_____
_____
_____
_____
_____
_____
_____
_____

My Dream

Date: _____ Title: _____ Is it a recurring dream? _____

_____
_____
_____
_____
_____
_____
_____
_____
_____
_____

> Dream Scape

What is the dream motif? _____

_____

My dream: _____

_____

_____

_____

_____

My Dream, cont'd.

_____
_____
_____
_____

About You

What time did you go to bed? _____

What did you eat before going to bed? _____

What did you watch, read, or listen to? _____

What kind of mood were you in? _____

What did you drink? _____

Did you take any medication? _____

What was your focus at the moment?

Relationship_____ Travel_____ Career_____ Abundance_____

Health_____ Other_____

My Conclusion

_____
_____
_____
_____
_____
_____
_____
_____
_____
_____
_____

My Dream

Date:_____ Title:_____ Is it a recurring dream?_____

Dream Scape

What is the dream motif?_____

My dream:_____

_____

_____

_____

_____

Quote

_____

_____

_____

_____

_____

_____

_____

_____

_____

_____

_____

_____
_____
_____
_____

About You

What time did you go to bed? _____

What did you eat before going to bed? _____

What did you watch, read, or listen to? _____

What kind of mood were you in? _____

What did you drink? _____

Did you take any medication? _____

What was your focus at the moment?

Relationship_____ Travel_____ Career_____ Abundance_____

Health_____ Other_____

My Conclusion

_____
_____
_____
_____
_____
_____
_____
_____
_____
_____
_____
_____

My Dream

Date:_____ Title:_____ Is it a recurring dream?_____

_____

Dream Scape

_____

_____

_____

_____

_____

_____

_____

_____

_____

_____

What is the dream motif?_____

My dream:_____

_____

_____

_____

_____

_____

_____

_____

_____

About You

What time did you go to bed? _____

What did you eat before going to bed? _____

What did you watch, read, or listen to? _____

What kind of mood were you in? _____

What did you drink? _____

Did you take any medication? _____

What was your focus at the moment?

Relationship_____ Travel_____ Career_____ Abundance_____

Health_____ Other_____

My Conclusion

_____

_____

_____

_____

_____

_____

_____

_____

_____

_____

_____

My Dream

Date:_____ Title:_____ Is it a recurring dream?_____

Dream Scape

What is the dream motif?_____

My dream:_____

My Dream, cont'd.

_____
_____
_____
_____

About You

What time did you go to bed? _____

What did you eat before going to bed? _____

What did you watch, read, or listen to? _____

What kind of mood were you in? _____

What did you drink? _____

Did you take any medication? _____

What was your focus at the moment?

Relationship_____Travel_____Career_____Abundance_____

Health_____Other_____

My Conclusion

_____
_____
_____
_____
_____
_____
_____
_____
_____
_____

My Dream

Date: _____ Title: _____ Is it a recurring dream? _____

_____

_____

_____

_____

_____

_____

_____

_____

_____

_____

Dream Scape

What is the dream motif? _____

_____

My dream: _____

_____

_____

_____

_____

_____

_____

_____

_____

About You

What time did you go to bed? _____

What did you eat before going to bed? _____

What did you watch, read, or listen to? _____

What kind of mood were you in? _____

What did you drink? _____

Did you take any medication? _____

What was your focus at the moment?

Relationship_____ Travel_____ Career_____ Abundance_____

Health_____ Other_____

My Conclusion

_____

_____

_____

_____

_____

_____

_____

_____

_____

_____

_____

_____

_____

My Dream

Date:_____ Title:_____ Is it a recurring dream?_____

Dream Scape

_____

_____

_____

_____

_____

_____

_____

_____

_____

_____

_____

What is the dream motif?_____

_____

My dream:_____

_____

_____

_____

_____

_____

_____

_____

_____

About You

What time did you go to bed? _____

What did you eat before going to bed? _____

What did you watch, read, or listen to? _____

What kind of mood were you in? _____

What did you drink? _____

Did you take any medication? _____

What was your focus at the moment?

Relationship_____ Travel_____ Career_____ Abundance_____

Health_____ Other_____

My Conclusion

_____

_____

_____

_____

_____

_____

_____

_____

_____

_____

_____

_____

My Dream

Date:_____ Title:_____ Is it a recurring dream?_____

Quote
_____
_____
_____
_____
_____
_____
_____
_____
_____
_____
_____

Dream Scape

What is the dream motif?_____

_____

My dream:_____
_____
_____
_____
_____

My Dream, cont'd.

_____
_____
_____
_____

About You

My Conclusion

What time did you go to bed? _____

What did you eat before going to bed? _____

What did you watch, read, or listen to? _____

What kind of mood were you in? _____

What did you drink? _____

Did you take any medication? _____

What was your focus at the moment?

Relationship_____ Travel_____ Career_____ Abundance_____

Health_____ Other_____

_____
_____
_____
_____
_____
_____
_____
_____
_____
_____
_____
_____

My Dream

Date:_____ Title:_____ Is it a recurring dream?_____

Dream Scape

What is the dream motif?_____

My dream:_____
_____
_____
_____
_____

_____
_____
_____
_____

About You

My Conclusion

What time did you go to bed?_____

What did you eat before going to bed?_____

What did you watch, read, or listen to?_____

What kind of mood were you in?_____

What did you drink?_____

Did you take any medication?_____

What was your focus at the moment?

Relationship____Travel____Career____Abundance____

Health____Other____

_____
_____
_____
_____
_____
_____
_____
_____
_____
_____
_____
_____
_____

My Dream

Date: _____ Title: _____ Is it a recurring dream? _____

Dream Scape

What is the dream motif? _____

My dream: _____

_____

_____

_____

_____

Quote

_____

_____

_____

_____

_____

_____

_____

_____

_____

_____

My Dream, cont'd.

_____

_____

_____

_____

About You

What time did you go to bed? _____

What did you eat before going to bed? _____

What did you watch, read, or listen to? _____

What kind of mood were you in? _____

What did you drink? _____

Did you take any medication? _____

What was your focus at the moment?

Relationship_____Travel_____Career_____Abundance_____

Health_____Other_____

My Conclusion

_____

_____

_____

_____

_____

_____

_____

_____

_____

_____

_____

About the Author

Leon Nacson (an avid dreamer) was born in Alexandra, Egypt, to Greek parents. He is the founder of *The Planet* newspaper, a well-established publication that covers environmental, health, and personal development issues. Leon facilitates seminars and workshops throughout Australia and Asia for such notable individuals as Louise Hay, Denise Linn, Shakti Gawain, Stuart Wilde, and Deepak Chopra. He can also be heard on Australia's number-one radio station as the resident dream coach. This is Leon's ninth book. He works in Sydney with his sons, Eli and Rhett; and lives with his wife, Colleen, and dog, Astor.

Other Books by Leon Nacson

Aromatherapy for Lovers and Dreamers
(co-authored with Judith White and Karen Downes)

Aromatherapy for Meditation and Contemplation
(co-authored with Judith White and Karen Downes)

Cards, Stars and Dreams
(co-authored with Matthew Favaloro)

Deepak Chopra: World of Infinite Possibilities

Dyer Straight

Dreamer's Guide to the Galaxy

I Must Be Dreaming

Interpreting Dreams A-Z

Simply Wilde (co-authored with Stuart Wilde)

Leon is compiling a new book that will feature dreams from people around the world. If you have an interesting dream you wish to share with others, email: **nacson@theplanet.com.au**

Hay House Lifestyles Titles

Flip Books

101 Ways to Happiness, by Louise L. Hay

101 Ways to Health and Healing, by Louise L. Hay

101 Ways to Romance, by Barbara De Angelis, Ph.D.

101 Ways to Transform Your Life,
  by Dr. Wayne W. Dyer

Books

A Garden of Thoughts, by Louise L. Hay

Aromatherapy A–Z, by Connie Higley, Alan Higley,
  and Pat Leatham

Colors & Numbers, by Louise L. Hay

Constant Craving A–Z, by Doreen Virtue, Ph.D.

Dream Journal, by Leon Nacson

Healing with Herbs and Home Remedies A–Z,
  by Hanna Kroeger

Heal Your Body A–Z, by Louise L. Hay

Home Design with Feng Shui A–Z,
  by Terah Kathryn Collins

Homeopathy A–Z, by Dana Ullman, M.P.H.

Interpreting Dreams A–Z, by Leon Nacson

Natural Gardening A–Z, by Donald Trotter, Ph.D.

You Can Heal Your Life, by Louise L. Hay

and

Power Thought Cards, by Louise L. Hay

All of the above titles
may be ordered by
calling Hay House at
the numbers on the
next page.

We hope you enjoyed this Hay House Lifestyles
book. If you would like to receive a free catalog fea-
turing additional Hay House books and products,
or if you would like information about the
Hay Foundation, please contact:

Hay House, Inc.
P.O. Box 5100
Carlsbad, CA 92018-5100

(760) 431-7695 or (800) 654-5126
(760) 431-6948 (fax) or (800) 650-5115 (fax)

Please visit the Hay House Website at:
www.hayhouse.com